D0831423

{ To: }

....

{ From: }

....

{ Date:}

....

© 2012 Christian Art Gifts, RSA
        Christian Art Gifts Inc., IL, USA

Designed by Christian Art Gifts

Images used under license from Shutterstock.com

Printed in China

ISBN 978-1-4321-0162-6

101
Words that Matter Most
for Teens

{ Contents }

{ Acceptance }

Ac-cep-tance/ək'sɛptəns/*noun*

1. The act or process of accepting. 2. The state of being accepted or acceptable. 3. Favorable reception. 4. Acknowledgment, approval, recognition.

Honor God by accepting each other,
as Christ has accepted you.
– *Romans 15:7* CEV –

"Those the Father has given Me will come to Me, and I will never reject them."
– *John 6:37* –

God welcomes everyone.
– *Romans 14:3* CEV –

Jesus accepts you the way you are, but loves you too much to leave you that way.
– Lee Venden –

{ Achievement }

A-chieve-ment/əˈtʃiːvmənt/*noun*

1. The act of accomplishing or finishing.
2. Something accomplished successfully, especially by means of exertion, skill, practice, or perseverance. 3. Accomplishment, triumph, performance, completion, realization.

With God's power working in us,
God can do much, much more
than anything we can ask or imagine.
– *Ephesians 3:20 NCV* –

We don't have the right to claim that
we have done anything on our own.
God gives us what it takes to do all that we do.
– *2 Corinthians 3:5 CEV* –

LORD, all our success is
because of what You have done.
– *Isaiah 26:12 NCV* –

Nothing great was ever achieved without enthusiasm.

– Ralph Waldo Emerson –

{ Admiration }

Ad–mi–ra–tion/ˌædməˈreɪʃən/*noun*

1. A feeling of pleasure, wonder, and approval.
2. An object of wonder and esteem. 3. Regard, respect, awe.

Do not be interested only in your own life,
but be interested in the lives of others.
– *Philippians 2:4 NCV* –

Stop and consider the
wonderful miracles of God!
– *Job 37:14* –

A sensible person wins admiration.
– *Proverbs 12:8* –

He that respects not is not respected.
– George Herbert –

{ Adventure }

Ad-ven-ture/əd'vɛntʃə/*noun*/*verb*

1. An undertaking or enterprise of a hazardous nature. 2. An unusual or exciting experience. 3. Participation in hazardous or exciting experiences. 4. To venture upon; undertake or try. 5. To take a risk. 6. Quest, journey, exploration, voyage.

At the end of the journey
we'll surely rest with God.
– *Hebrews 4:10* MSG –

Your life is a journey you must
travel with a deep consciousness of God.
– *1 Peter 1:18* MSG –

Point out the road I must travel;
I'm all ears, all eyes before You.
– *Psalm 143:8* MSG –

Do not follow where the path may lead. Go instead where there is no path and leave a trail.
– Ralph Waldo Emerson –

{ Advice }

Ad–vice/əd'vaɪs/*noun*

1. Opinion about what could or should be done about a situation or problem. 2. Counsel, recommendation, suggestion, opinion.

Only God has wisdom and power,
good advice and understanding.
– *Job 12:13* NCV –

Your advice has been my guide,
and later You will welcome me in glory.
– *Psalm 73:24* CEV –

God gives helpful advice to
everyone who obeys Him.
– *Proverbs 2:7* CEV –

No gift is more precious than good advice.
– Desiderius Erasmus –

{ Affection }

Af-fec-tion/əˈfɛkʃən/*noun*

1. A tender feeling or emotion toward another.
2. A disposition to feel, do, or say. 3. Fondness, love, liking.

My dear children, let's not just
talk about love; let's practice real love.
– 1 John 3:19 MSG –

Love each other with genuine affection.
– Romans 12:10 –

I pray that your love will overflow
more and more, and that you will keep
on growing in knowledge and understanding.
– Philippians 1:9 –

Whatever a person may be like, we must still
love them because we love God.

– John Calvin –

{ Ambition }

Am–bi–tion/æm'bɪʃən/*noun*

1. An eager or strong desire to achieve something. 2. The object or goal desired. 3. Aspiration, dreams.

"Seek first God's kingdom and what God wants.
Then all your other needs will be met as well."
– *Matthew 6:33* NCV –

Try your best to live quietly, to mind
your own business, and to work hard.
– *1 Thessalonians 4:11* CEV –

Depend on the LORD and His strength;
always go to Him for help.
– *1 Chronicles 16:11* NCV –

I am only one, but still I am one. I cannot do
everything, but still I can do something; I will
not refuse to do the something I can do.
– Helen Keller –

{ Appearance }

Ap-pear-ance/ əˈpɪərəns/*noun*

1. The outward or visible aspect of a person or thing. 2. Look, visual aspect.

God does not see the same way people see.
People look at the outside of a person,
but the LORD looks at the heart.
– *1 Samuel 16:7 NCV* –

We justify our actions by appearances;
God examines our motives.
– *Proverbs 21:2 MSG* –

Stop judging by the way things look,
but judge by what is really right.
– *John 7:24 NCV* –

Appearances are often deceiving.

– Aesop –

{ Approval }

Ap–prov–al/əˈpruːvəl/*noun*

1. The act or an instance of approving.
2. Favorable regard. 3. Endorsement, consent.

There's trouble ahead when you live only
for the approval of others, saying what
flatters them, doing what indulges them.
– *Luke 6:26* MSG –

When God approves of your life, even your
enemies will end up shaking your hand.
– *Proverbs 16:7* MSG –

No one can do anything
without the Lord's approval.
– *Lamentations 3:37* CEV –

Desire for approval and recognition is a
healthy motive.

– Albert Einstein –

{ Assurance }

As–sur–ance/əˈʃʊərəns/*noun*

1. The act of assuring. 2. A statement or indication that inspires confidence. 3. Freedom from doubt. 4. Courage, guarantee, certainty.

Christ lives in you. This gives you
assurance of sharing His glory.
– Colossians 1:27 –

Christ has given us much
assurance of a better agreement.
– Hebrews 8:6 CEV –

The Spirit also makes us sure that we
will be given what God has stored up
for His people. Then we will be set free,
and God will be honored and praised.
– Ephesians 1:14 CEV –

The wise Christian will not let his assurance
depend upon his powers of imagination.
– A. W. Tozer –

{ Attitude }

At-ti-tude/ˈætɪˌtjuːd/*noun*

1. A state of mind or a feeling. 2. The way a person views something or tends to behave towards it. 3. Mentality, mindset, outlook, esteem, respect, regard.

May the patience and encouragement that come from God allow you to live in harmony with each other the way Christ Jesus wants.
– Romans 15:5 NCV –

Be tenderhearted, and keep a humble attitude.
– 1 Peter 3:8 –

Let the Spirit renew your thoughts and attitudes.
– Ephesians 4:23 –

A positive attitude will have positive results because attitudes are contagious.
– Zig Ziglar –

{ Authority }

Au–thor–i–ty /ɔːˈθɒrɪtɪ/ *noun*

1. The power to enforce laws, exact obedience, command, determine, or judge. 2. An accepted source of expert information or advice.
3. Power, right, ability, control, command.

Obey the rulers who have authority over you.
Only God can give authority to anyone,
and He puts these rulers in their places of power.
– Romans 13:1 CEV –

Obey your leaders and act under their authority.
They are watching over you, because
they are responsible for your souls.
– Hebrews 13:17 NCV –

"By My power I will make My people strong,
and by My authority they will go wherever
they wish. I, the LORD, have spoken!"
– Zechariah 10:12 –

The wisest have the most authority.

– Plato –

{ Bible }

Bi–ble /ˈbaɪbəl/ *noun*

1. The inspired Word of God in Christianity that comprises the books of the Old and New Testaments. 2. Guides Christians in living a life that glorifies God. 3. Good Book, Holy Scripture, Scripture, Word of God.

In the beginning there was the Word.
The Word was with God, and the Word was God.
– John 1:1 NCV –

Everything in the Scriptures is
God's Word. All of it is useful for teaching
and helping people and for correcting
them and showing them how to live.
– 2 Timothy 3:16 CEV –

God's Word is alive and working and
is sharper than a double-edged sword.
– Hebrews 4:12 NCV –

The Bible is the best gift God has given to man.
— Abraham Lincoln —

{ Blessings }

Bless–ings/ˈblɛsɪŋs/*noun*

1. The act of one that blesses. 2. Something promoting or contributing to happiness, well-being, or prosperity. 3. Approval, permission.

I pray that God will take care of all your
needs with the wonderful blessings
that come from Christ Jesus!
– *Philippians 4:19* CEV –

Praise the God and Father of our
Lord Jesus Christ for the spiritual blessings
that Christ has brought us from heaven!
– *Ephesians 1:3* CEV –

Every good and perfect gift comes
down from the Father who created all the
lights in the heavens. He is always the same.
– *James 1:17* CEV –

God is more anxious to bestow His blessings
on us than we are to receive them.
– St. Augustine –

{ Certainty }

Cer–tain–ty /ˈsɜːtəntɪ/ *noun*

1. The fact, quality, or state of being certain.
2. Something that is clearly established or assured. 3. Confidence, assurance, sureness.

We know it for sure. Jesus
is the Savior of the world!
– *John 4:39* MSG –

Be cheerful. Keep things in good repair.
Keep your spirits up. Think in harmony.
Be agreeable. Do all that, and the God of
love and peace will be with you for sure.
– *2 Corinthians 13:11* MSG –

"I tell you for certain that everyone
who has faith in Me has eternal life."
– *John 6:47* CEV –

We must meet the uncertainties of this world
with the certainty of the world to come.
– A. W. Tozer –

{ Challenges }

Chal-lenges/ˈtʃælɪndʒ/*noun*

1. A test of one's abilities or resources in a demanding but stimulating undertaking.
2. State of affairs, trial.

Consider it a sheer gift, friends, when tests
and challenges come at you from all sides.
You know that under pressure, your faith-life
is forced into the open and shows its true colors.
— James 1:2-3 MSG —

LORD, try me and test me;
look closely into my heart and mind.
— Psalm 26:2 NCV —

Troubles come to prove that your faith is pure.
— 1 Peter 1:7 NCV —

Unless a man undertakes more than he
possibly can do, he will never do all that
he can.

— Henry Drummond —

{ Change }

Change /tʃeɪndʒ/ *noun*

1. The act, process, or result of altering or modifying. 2. A transformation or transition from one state, condition, or phase to another. 3. Something different. 4. Alteration, modification, variation, transformation, adjustment.

What the LORD has planned will stand forever.
His thoughts never change.
– *Psalm 33:11* CEV –

"I am the LORD, and I do not change."
– *Malachi 3:6* –

"Change your hearts and lives
because the kingdom of heaven is near."
– *Matthew 3:2* NCV –

Lord, when we are wrong, make us willing to change.

– Peter Marshall –

{ Character }

Char–ac–ter/ˈkærɪktə/*noun/adjective*

1. The combination of qualities or features that distinguishes one person from another.
2. Moral or ethical strength. 3. A description of a person's attributes, traits, or abilities.
4. Quality, property, personality, reputation.

Endurance develops strength
of character, and character strengthens
our confident hope of salvation.
– Romans 5:4 –

"God blesses those whose hearts
are pure, for they will see God."
– Matthew 5:8 –

May you always be filled with the fruit
of your salvation – the righteous character
produced in your life by Jesus Christ.
– Philippians 1:11 –

Character is what you are in the dark.
– Dwight L. Moody –

{ Church }

Church /tʃɜːtʃ/ *noun*

1. The body of people who attend or belong to a particular local church. 2. A body of believers who gather to worship and pray. 3. Congregation, fellowship, fold, parish.

The church is Christ's body, in which
He speaks and acts, by which He
fills everything with His presence.
– *Ephesians 1:20 MSG* –

You should not stay away from the church
meetings, as some are doing, but you should
meet together and encourage each other.
– *Hebrews 10:25 NCV* –

The church of the living God
is the strong foundation of truth.
– *1 Timothy 3:15 CEV* –

Every Christian's place is in a local church …
sharing in its worship, its fellowship, and its
witness.

– John R. W. Stott –

{ Communication }

Com-mu-ni-ca-tion/kəˌmjuːnɪˈkeɪʃən/*noun*

1. The act of communicating. 2. The exchange of thoughts, messages, or information, as by speech, signals, writing, or behavior. 3. Interpersonal rapport. 4. The art and technique of using words effectively to impart information or ideas. 5. Discussion, discourse, expression, message.

When you talk, do not say harmful things, but say what people need – words that will help others become stronger. Then what you say will do good to those who listen to you.
– Ephesians 4:29 NCV –

The LORD reached out His hand and touched my mouth. He said to me, "See, I am putting My words in your mouth."
– Jeremiah 1:9 NCV –

Share every good thing you have with anyone who teaches you what God has said.
– Galatians 6:6 CEV –

Every generation of Christians has this problem of learning how to speak meaningfully to its own age.
– Francis Schaeffer –

{ Compassion }

Com-pas-sion/kəmˈpæʃən/*noun*

1. Deep awareness of the suffering of another coupled with the wish to relieve it. 2. Pity, mercy, sympathy.

Be kind to each other, tenderhearted,
forgiving one another.
– Ephesians 4:32 –

The LORD replied, "I will show
mercy to anyone I choose, and I will
show compassion to anyone I choose."
– Exodus 33:19 –

By helping each other with your troubles,
you truly obey the law of Christ.
– Galatians 6:2 NCV –

Let all find compassion in you.
– John of the Cross –

{ Confidence }

Con–fi–dence/ˈkɒnfɪdəns/*noun*

1. Trust or faith in a person or thing. 2. A feeling of assurance, especially of self-assurance. 3. The state or quality of being certain. 4. Sureness, certainty, trust.

I have confidence from the Lord.
– *Philippians 2:24* –

In quietness and confidence is your strength.
– *Isaiah 30:15* –

Blessed are those who trust in the LORD and have made the LORD their hope and confidence.
– *Jeremiah 17:7* –

Nothing can be done without hope and confidence.

— Helen Keller —

{ Courage }

Cour–age/ˈkʌrɪdʒ/*noun*

**1. The state or quality of mind or spirit that enables one to face danger or fear with self-possession, confidence, and resolution.
2. Bravery, spirit, heart, fearless.**

Do not be afraid or discouraged. For the LORD
your God is with you wherever you go.
– *Joshua 1:9* –

Be strong and courageous, all you
who put your hope in the LORD!
– *Psalm 31:24* –

Be on guard. Stand firm in the faith.
Be courageous.
– *1 Corinthians 16:13* –

It takes courage to grow up and become who
you really are.

– E. W. Cummings –

{ Decisions }

De-ci-sions /dɪˈsɪʒənz/ *noun*

1. The passing of judgment on an issue under consideration. 2. The act of reaching a conclusion or making up one's mind. 3. Judgment reached or pronounced. 4. Choice, conclusion, verdict.

The LORD will be with you
when you make a decision.
– *2 Chronicles 19:6 NCV* –

We make our own decisions, but the
LORD alone determines what happens.
– *Proverbs 16:33 CEV* –

Let's decide for ourselves what is right,
and let's learn together what is good.
– *Job 34:4 NCV* –

When you have to make a choice and don't make it, that in itself is a choice.

– William James –

{ Dependability }

De–pend–a–bil–i–ty/dɪˈpɛndəbəlɪtɪ/*noun*

1. The quality of being reliable or dependable.
2. Deserving of trust or confidence. 3. Faithfulness, reliability, trustworthiness.

Try your best to please God and to be like Him.
Be faithful, loving, dependable, and gentle.
– 1 Timothy 6:11 CEV –

Know this: God, your God, is a God
indeed, a God you can depend upon.
– Deuteronomy 7:7 MSG –

We depend on You, LORD,
to help and protect us.
– Psalm 33:20 CEV –

You may depend on the Lord, but can He
depend on you?

– Croft M. Pentz –

{ Determination }

De-ter-mi-na-tion/dɪˌtɜːmɪ'neɪʃən/*noun*

1. A fixed intention or resolution. 2. A fixed movement or tendency toward an object or end. 3. Willpower, purpose.

I am determined to keep Your
decrees to the very end.
– *Psalm 119:112* –

We must be determined to run
the race that is ahead of us.
– *Hebrews 12:1* CEV –

Stand firm and don't be shaken.
Always keep busy working for the Lord.
You know that everything you
do for Him is worthwhile.
– *1 Corinthians 15:58* CEV –

Most men succeed because they are determined to.

– George Allen –

{ Discipline }

Dis–ci–pline/ˈdɪsɪplɪn/*noun*

1. Training expected to produce a specific character or pattern of behavior, especially training that produces moral or mental improvement. 2. Controlled behavior resulting from disciplinary training. 3. Trait, restraint, self-control.

We do not enjoy being disciplined.
It is painful at the time, but later, after
we have learned from it, we have peace,
because we start living in the right way.
– *Hebrews 12:11* NCV –

Hold on through your sufferings,
because they are like a father's discipline.
God is treating you as children.
All children are disciplined by their fathers.
– *Hebrews 12:7* NCV –

Teach me to do Your will, for You are my God.
May Your gracious Spirit lead me forward.
– *Psalm 143:10* –

The best discipline, maybe the only discipline
that really works, is self-discipline.
– Walter Kiechel III –

{ Emotions }

E-mo-tions /ɪˈməʊʃəns/ *noun*

1. A mental state that arises spontaneously rather than through conscious effort and is often accompanied by physiological changes. 2. The part of the consciousness that involves feeling. 3. Feeling, sentiment, sensation.

Pour out your feelings to the LORD,
as you would pour water out of a jug.
– *Lamentations 2:19* CEV –

Those who belong to Christ Jesus
have given up their old selfish feelings.
– *Galatians 5:24* NCV –

God is greater than our feelings,
and He knows everything.
– *1 John 3:20* –

People are moved and motivated by emotions.
– Robert Conklin –

{ Encouragement }

En–cour–age–ment/ɪnˈkʌrɪdʒmənt/*noun*

1. The act of encouraging. 2. The state of being encouraged. 3. Approval, promotion, assistance, boost.

May our Lord Jesus Christ Himself and God our Father encourage you and strengthen you in every good thing you do and say. God loved us, and through His grace He gave us a good hope and encouragement that continues forever.
– *2 Thessalonians 2:16-17 NCV* –

Be strong and courageous! Do not be afraid.
– *Deuteronomy 31:6* –

Let all who seek God's help be encouraged.
– *Psalm 69:32* –

The really great man is the man who makes every man feel great.

– G. K. Chesterton –

{ Entertainment }

En–ter–tain–ment/ˌɛntəˈteɪnmənt/*noun*

1. The act of entertaining. 2. The art or field of entertaining. 3. Something that amuses, pleases, or diverts, especially a performance or show. 4. The pleasure afforded by being entertained. 5. Amusement, leisure, recreation.

Take care of yourself, have a good time, and make the most of whatever job you have for as long as God gives you life.
– *Ecclesiastes 5:18* MSG –

Young people eventually reveal by their actions if their motives are on the up and up.
– *Proverbs 20:11* MSG –

Hate what is wrong. Hold tightly to what is good.
– *Romans 12:9* –

If you are losing your leisure, look out! You are losing your soul.

– Logan Pearsall Smith –

{ Eternity }

E–ter–ni–ty /ɪˈtɜːnɪtɪ/ *noun*

1. Time without beginning or end. 2. The state or quality of being eternal. 3. The timeless state following death. 4. A very long or seemingly endless time. 5. Infinity, forever, timeless.

God has planted eternity in the human heart, but even so, people cannot see the whole scope of God's work from beginning to end.
– Ecclesiastes 3:11 –

"From eternity to eternity I am God."
– Isaiah 43:13 –

"Everyone who has faith in the Son of Man will have eternal life."
– John 3:15 CEV –

Eternity is the place where questions and answers become one.

– Eli Wiessel –

{ Example }

Ex-am-ple/ɪgˈzɑːmpəl/*noun*

1. One that is representative of a group as a whole. 2. One serving as a pattern of a specific kind. 3. Illustration, model, representation.

Don't let anyone make fun of you,
just because you are young. Set an example
for other followers by what you say and do.
– *1 Timothy 4:12* CEV –

"Here is a simple rule of thumb for behavior:
Ask yourself what you want people to do for you;
then grab the initiative and do it for them!"
– *Luke 6:31* MSG –

Follow my example,
as I follow the example of Christ.
– *1 Corinthians 11:1* NCV –

The first great gift we can bestow on others is a good example.

– Thomas Morell –

{ Excellence }

Ex–cel–lence/'ɛksələns/*noun*

1. The state, quality, or condition of excelling.
2. Quality, impressiveness, superiority.

Fix your thoughts on what is true,
and honorable, and right, and pure, and
lovely, and admirable. Think about things
that are excellent and worthy of praise.
– *Philippians 4:8* –

Everyone who has been wise will shine as
bright as the sky above, and everyone who has
led others to please God will shine like the stars.
– *Daniel 12:3* CEV –

The righteous keep moving forward, and those
with clean hands become stronger and stronger.
– *Job 17:9* –

> We are what we repeatedly do. Excellence,
> then, is not an act but a habit.
>
> – Aristotle –

{ Fairness }

Fair–ness/fɛənɪs/*noun*

1. Free from favoritism, self-interest, or preference in judgment. 2. Conformity with rules or standards. 3. Ability to make judgments free from discrimination or dishonesty. 4. Justice, equality.

The LORD loves justice and fairness, and
He is kind to everyone everywhere on earth.
– Psalm 33:5 CEV –

The LORD demands accurate scales and
balances; He sets the standards for fairness.
– Proverbs 16:11 –

Good people speak with wisdom,
and they say what is fair.
– Psalm 37:30 NCV –

It is not fair to ask of others what you are not willing to do yourself.

— Eleanor Roosevelt —

{ Faith }

Faith /feɪθ/ *noun*

1. The belief that God is always present and able to help and guide His children. 2 Trust in God and His promises. 3 Belief, devotion, religion.

Faith means being sure of the things
we hope for and knowing that something
is real even if we do not see it.
– *Hebrews 11:1 NCV* –

Fight the good fight for the
true faith. Hold tightly to the eternal
life to which God has called you.
– *1 Timothy 6:12* –

"Anything is possible for
someone who has faith!"
– *Mark 9:23 CEV* –

Faith makes all things possible ... love makes all things easy.

– Dwight L. Moody –

{ Family }

Fam-i-ly/'fæmɪlɪ/*noun*

1. A fundamental social group in society typically consisting of one or two parents and their children. 2. All the members of a household under one roof. 3. Household, home, social unit, kin, homefolk.

"I will be your Father, and you will be My sons and daughters," says the LORD Almighty.
– 2 Corinthians 6:18 –

You belong to God's family.
– Ephesians 2:19 NCV –

I pray that the LORD will let your family and your descendants always grow strong.
– Psalm 115:14 CEV –

We never know the love of our parents for us till we have become parents.

– Henry Ward Beecher –

{ Father }

Fa-ther/ˈfɑːðə/*noun*

1. A man who raises a child. 2. A male parent.
3. God. 4. The first person of the Christian
Trinity.

Ten thousand people may teach you about
Christ, but I am your only Father. You became
My children when I told you about Christ Jesus.
– *1 Corinthians 4:15* CEV –

You have one Father, who is in heaven.
– *Matthew 23:9* NCV –

The LORD is like a father to His children,
tender and compassionate.
– *Psalm 103:13* –

The greatest thing a man can do for his
Heavenly Father is to be kind to some of His
other children.

– Henry Drummond –

{ Forgiveness }

For-give-ness /fə'gɪvnɪs/ *noun*

1. The act of forgiving. 2. Pardon, mercy, amnesty, acquittal, exoneration.

God made you alive with Christ,
and He forgave all our sins.
– *Colossians 2:13 NCV* –

If we confess our sins, He will forgive our sins,
because we can trust God to do what is right. He
will cleanse us from all the wrongs we have done.
– *1 John 1:9 NCV* –

The LORD has taken our sins away
from us as far as the east is from west.
– *Psalm 103:12 NCV* –

To err is human, to forgive, divine.

– Alexander Pope –

{ Freedom }

Free-dom /ˈfriːdəm/ *noun*

1. The condition of being free of restraints.
2. Exemption from an unpleasant or onerous condition. 3. A right or the power to engage in certain actions without control or interference. 4. Liberty, free will.

You must be careful so that your
freedom does not cause others
with a weaker conscience to stumble.
– 1 Corinthians 8:9 –

Exercise your freedom by serving
God, not by breaking the rules.
Treat everyone you meet with dignity.
– 1 Peter 2:16 MSG –

Christ has set us free! This means we are
really free. Now hold on to your freedom.
– Galatians 5:1 CEV –

We find freedom when we find God; we lose it
when we lose Him.

– Paul E. Scherer –

{ Friendship }

Friend–ship/frɛndʃɪp/*noun*

1. The quality or condition of being friends.
2. A friendly relationship. 3. Relationship, alliance, goodwill, affinity, closeness, companionship, amity, friendliness.

Friends love through all kinds of weather,
and families stick together in all kinds of trouble.
– *Proverbs 17:17 MSG* –

Friends come and friends go,
but a true friend sticks by you like family.
– *Proverbs 18:24 MSG* –

As iron sharpens iron,
so a friend sharpens a friend.
– *Proverbs 27:17* –

The only way to have a friend is to be one.
– Ralph Waldo Emerson –

{ Future }

Fu–ture/ˈfjuːtʃə/*noun*

1. The indefinite time yet to come. 2. Something that will happen in time to come. 3. A prospective or expected condition, especially one considered with regard to growth, advancement, or development. 4. Hereafter, tomorrow.

"I know the plans I have for you," says the LORD.
"They are plans for good and not for disaster,
to give you a future and a hope."
– Jeremiah 29:11 –

You will have hope for the future,
and your wishes will come true.
– Proverbs 23:18 NCV –

Your future will be brighter by far than your past.
– Job 8:7 CEV –

Never be afraid to trust an unknown future to a known God.

— Corrie ten Boom —

{ Generosity }

Gen–er–os–i–ty /ˌdʒɛnəˈrɒsɪtɪ/ *noun*

1. Liberality in giving or willingness to give.
2. Nobility of thought or behavior. 3. A generous act. 4. Kindness, charity.

"If you give to others, you will be given a full amount in return. It will be packed down, shaken together, and spilling over into your lap. The way you treat others is the way you will be treated."
– Luke 6:38 CEV –

The generous will prosper; those who refresh others will themselves be refreshed.
– Proverbs 11:25 –

Generous people plan to do what is generous, and they stand firm in their generosity.
– Isaiah 32:8 –

Generosity always wins favor, particularly when accompanied by modesty.
– Johann Wolfgang von Goethe –

{ Goals }

Goals /gəʊls/ *noun*

1. The purpose toward which an endeavor is directed. 2. End, objective, aim, target, intention.

This command I give you today is not too hard for you; it is not beyond what you can do.
– *Deuteronomy 30:11 NCV* –

Our only goal is to please God.
– *2 Corinthians 5:9 NCV* –

It is pleasant to see dreams come true.
– *Proverbs 13:19* –

If you aim at nothing, you will hit it every time.
– Zig Ziglar –

{ God }

God/gɒd/*noun*

1. Our Heavenly Father who created the universe and gave human beings all they need to live a life to His honor. 2. He is the source of life and our hope and safety in times of adversity. 3. The creator and ruler of the world. 4. Almighty, Jehovah, Abba, Great I AM, Lord.

O nations of the world, recognize the LORD, recognize that the LORD is glorious and strong.
– 1 Chronicles 16:28 –

God created everything in the
heavenly realms and on earth.
– Colossians 1:16 –

Everything God has done will last forever;
nothing He does can ever be changed. God
has done all this, so that we will worship Him.
– Ecclesiastes 3:14 CEV –

> Don't think so much about who is for or
> against you, rather give all your care that God
> be with you in everything you do.
> – Thomas à Kempis –

{ Gratitude }

Grat–i–tude/ˈɡrætɪˌtjuːd/*noun*

1. The state of being grateful. 2. Thankfulness, appreciation.

We should be grateful that we were given a kingdom that cannot be shaken. And in this kingdom we please God by worshiping Him and by showing Him great honor and respect.
– *Hebrews 12:28* CEV –

Be thankful in all circumstances, for this is God's will for you who belong to Christ Jesus.
– *1 Thessalonians 5:18* –

Since everything God created is good, we should not reject any of it but receive it with thanks.
– *1 Timothy 4:4* –

This day and your life are God's gift to you: so give thanks and be joyful always!
– Jim Beggs –

{ Guidance }

Guid-ance/'gaɪdəns/*noun*

1. The act or process of guiding. 2. Counseling, direction.

The Lord says, "I will make you wise
and show you where to go. I will
guide you and watch over you."
– *Psalm 32:8* NCV –

God is our God forever and ever.
He will guide us from now on.
– *Psalm 48:14* NCV –

The LORD will always guide you.
– *Isaiah 58:11* CEV –

Where God guides, He provides.

– Anonymous –

{ Happiness }

Hap-pi-ness/'hæpɪnɪs/*noun*

1. Enjoying, showing, or marked by pleasure, satisfaction, or joy. 2. Cheerfulness, gladness, delight.

May the LORD bless His people with peace and happiness and let them celebrate.
– *Psalm 64:10* CEV –

Give me happiness, O Lord,
for I give myself to You.
– *Psalm 86:4* –

Always be joyful.
– *1 Thessalonians 5:16* –

Whoever is happy will make others happy too.
– Anne Frank –

{ Help }

Help/hɛlp/*noun*

1. The act or an instance of helping. 2. Aid or assistance. 3. A person employed to help.

My help comes from the LORD,
who made heaven and earth!
– *Psalm 121:1* –

God is our mighty fortress,
always ready to help in times of trouble.
– *Psalm 46:1* CEV –

The LORD is good, a strong refuge when trouble
comes. He is close to those who trust in Him.
– *Nahum 1:7* –

Do something for those who have need of
help, something for which you get no pay but
the privilege of doing it.

– Albert Schweitzer –

{ Home }

Home /həʊm/ *noun*

1. A place where one lives. 2. A dwelling place together with the family or social unit that occupies it. 3. An environment offering security and happiness. 4. A valued place regarded as a refuge. 5. Residence, homestead.

God will have a house for us. It will not be
a house made by human hands; instead, it will
be a home in heaven that will last forever.
– 2 Corinthians 5:1 NCV –

This world is not our permanent home;
we are looking forward to a home yet to come.
– Hebrews 13:14 –

The LORD will bless the
home of those who do right.
– Proverbs 3:33 NCV –

God will never, never, never let us down if we
have faith and put our trust in Him. He will
always look after us.

— Mother Teresa —

{ Honesty }

Hon-es-ty/'ɒnɪstɪ/*noun*

1. The quality or condition of being honest.
2. Telling the truth. 3. Integrity, truthfulness, sincerity.

Look at those who are honest
and good, for a wonderful future
awaits those who love peace.
– *Psalm 37:37* –

What joy for those whose record
the LORD has cleared of guilt, whose
lives are lived in complete honesty!
– *Psalm 32:2* –

Your honesty will protect you
as you advance, and the glory of the
·LORD will defend you from behind.
– *Isaiah 58:8* CEV –

Honesty is the first chapter of the book of wisdom.

– Thomas Jefferson –

{ Hope }

Hope/həʊp/*verb/noun*

1. To wish for something with expectation of its fulfillment. 2. A wish or desire accompanied by confident expectation of its fulfillment. 3. The theological virtue defined as the desire and search for a future good, difficult but not impossible to attain with God's help. 4. Trust, confidence, anticipation, expectancy.

I pray that God, the source of hope,
will fill you completely with joy and
peace because you trust in Him. Then
you will overflow with confident hope.
– *Romans 15:13* –

There is one body and one Spirit,
and God called you to have one hope.
– *Ephesians 4:4 NCV* –

The LORD is good to those who
hope in Him, to those who seek Him.
– *Lamentations 3:25 NCV* –

Without Christ there is no hope.
– Charles H. Spurgeon –

{ Humility }

Hu–mil–i–ty/hjuːˈmɪlɪtɪ/*noun*

1. The quality or condition of being humble.
2. Humbleness, meekness.

Be humble in the presence of
God's mighty power, and He will
honor you when the time comes.
– *1 Peter 5:6* CEV –

Don't be selfish; don't try to
impress others. Be humble, thinking
of others as better than yourselves.
– *Philippians 2:3* –

Humble yourselves before the Lord,
and He will lift you up in honor.
– *James 4:10* –

Humility is strong, not bold; quiet, not
speechless; sure, not arrogant.

– Estelle Smith –

{ Identity }

I–den–ti–ty /aɪˈdɛntɪtɪ/ *noun*

1. The distinct personality of an individual regarded as a persisting entity. 2. Individuality, uniqueness, distinctiveness, personality.

"Live out your God-created identity.
Live generously and graciously toward
others, the way God lives toward you."
– *Matthew 5:48 MSG* –

You are God's child, and God will give you the
blessing He promised, because you are His child.
– *Galatians 4:7 NCV* –

You are God's chosen ones,
and He will bless you.
– *1 Peter 3:9 CEV* –

Being at peace with yourself is a direct result
of finding peace with God.

– Anonymous –

{ Independence }

In–de–pen–dence /ˌɪndɪˈpɛndəns/ *noun*

1. The state or quality of being independent.
2. Freedom, autonomy, self-sufficiency, liberty.

Trust God from the bottom of your heart;
don't try to figure out everything on your own.
– Proverbs 3:5 MSG –

"I am the LORD All-Powerful.
So don't depend on your own power
or strength, but on My Spirit."
– Zechariah 4:6 CEV –

You were saved by faith in God,
who treats us much better than we deserve.
This is God's gift to you, and not
anything you have done on your own.
– Ephesians 2:8 CEV –

> One can endure sorrow alone, but it takes two
> to be glad.
>
> **– Elbert Hubbard –**

54

{ Integrity }

In-teg-ri-ty/ɪnˈtɛgrɪtɪ/*noun*

1. Steadfast adherence to a strict moral or ethical code. 2. Character, honesty.

I know, my God, that You examine our hearts
and rejoice when You find integrity there.
– *1 Chronicles 29:17* –

Let God weigh me on the scales
of justice, for He knows my integrity.
– *Job 31:6* –

The honest person will live in safety,
but the dishonest will be caught.
– *Proverbs 10:9 NCV* –

Integrity is the noblest possession.
– Latin Proverb –

{ Intelligence }

In-tel-li-gence/ɪnˈtɛlɪdʒəns/*noun*

1. The capacity to acquire and apply knowledge. 2. The faculty of thought and reason. 3. Superior powers of mind. 4. Brainpower, brilliance, genius, intellect, cleverness.

"Love the Lord your God with all your passion and prayer and intelligence."
– *Matthew 22:37* MSG –

An intelligent person is always eager to take in more truth.
– *Proverbs 15:14* MSG –

Don't destroy yourself by being too good or acting too smart!
– *Ecclesiastes 7:16* CEV –

Genius is 99% perspiration and 1% inspiration.

– Thomas Edison –

{ Jesus }

Je–sus /'dʒiːzəs/ *noun*

**1. God's only Son and our Lord, who sacrificed His life on the cross to save us from sin.
2. Savior, Immanuel, Good Shepherd, Alpha and Omega, Bread of Life, Christ, King of kings, Lord of lords, Lamb of God, Light of the world, Messiah.**

No one can see God,
but Jesus Christ is exactly like Him.
– *Colossians 1:15 NCV* –

Jesus Christ is the same
yesterday, today, and forever.
– *Hebrews 13:8 NCV* –

Christ offered His life's blood as a
sacrifice and brought you near God.
– *Ephesians 2:13 CEV* –

If ever man was God or God man, Jesus Christ was both.

– Lord Byron –

{ Kindness }

Kind-ness/'kaɪndnɪs/*noun*

1. The quality or state of being kind. 2. An instance of kind behavior. 3. Generosity.

I will sing to You, LORD!
I will celebrate Your kindness and Your justice.
– *Psalm 101:1 CEV* –

God has us where He wants us, with all the
time in this world and the next to shower
grace and kindness upon us in Christ Jesus.
– *Ephesians 2:7 MSG* –

Let everyone see that you are gentle and kind.
– *Philippians 4:5 NCV* –

Three things in human life are important. The
first is to be kind. The second is to be kind.
The third is to be kind.

– Henry James –

{ Knowledge }

Knowl-edge/ˈnɒlɪdʒ/*noun*

1. The state or fact of knowing. 2. Familiarity, awareness, or understanding gained through experience or study. 3. The sum or range of what has been perceived, discovered, or learned. 4. Specific information about something.

Only the LORD gives wisdom;
He gives knowledge and understanding.
– *Proverbs 2:6 NCV* –

We sometimes tend to think we know
all we need to know to answer these kinds
of questions – but sometimes our humble
hearts can help us more than our proud minds.
– *1 Corinthians 8:1 MSG* –

God gives wisdom, knowledge,
and joy to those who please Him.
– *Ecclesiastes 2:26* –

He who lives up to a little knowledge shall have more knowledge.

– Thomas Brooks –

{ Love }

Love /lʌv/ *noun* / *verb*

1. A deep, tender feeling of affection toward a person, such as that arising from kinship, recognition of attractive qualities, or a sense of underlying oneness. 2. A feeling of intense desire and attraction toward a person. 3. An intense emotional attachment. 4. To experience deep affection or intense desire for another. 5. Emotion, adoration, affection, passion, caring.

We should love one another.
– *1 John 3:11* –

Love is more important than anything else.
It is what ties everything completely together.
– *Colossians 3:14* CEV –

Anyone who does not love does
not know God, for God is love.
– *1 John 4:8* –

Love is all we have, the only way that each can help the other.

– Euripides –

{ Loyalty }

Loy–al–ty/'lɔɪəltɪ/*noun*

1. The state or quality of being loyal. 2. A feeling or attitude of devoted attachment and affection. 3. Faithfulness, fidelity, allegiance, devotion.

The LORD gives His own reward
for doing good and for being loyal.
– *1 Samuel 26:23* –

Love the LORD, all you godly ones!
For the LORD protects
those who are loyal to Him.
– *Psalm 31:23* –

Create in me a clean heart, O God.
Renew a loyal spirit within me.
– *Psalm 51:10* –

Our loyalty is due not to our species but to God … it is spiritual, not biological, kinship that counts.

– C. S. Lewis –

{ Models }

Mod-els/mɒdəls/*noun*

1. People who serve as models in a particular behavioral or social role for another person to emulate. 2. Example.

Follow the example of good
people and live an honest life.
– *Proverbs 2:20* CEV –

Good people live right, and God blesses
the children who follow their example.
– *Proverbs 20:7* CEV –

Imitate me, just as I imitate Christ.
– *1 Corinthians 11:1* –

A pint of example is worth a gallon of advice.
– Anonymous –

{ Money }

Mon–ey/ˈmʌnɪ/*noun*

1. The official currency, coins, and negotiable paper notes issued by a government. 2. An amount of cash. 3. Cash, funds, riches, wealth.

Keep your lives free form the love of money
and be satisfied with what you have.
– Hebrews 13:5 NCV –

It is a good thing to receive wealth
from God and the good health to enjoy it.
To enjoy your work and accept your lot
in life – this is indeed a gift from God.
– Ecclesiastes 5:19 –

Honor the LORD with your wealth and with
the best part of everything you produce.
– Proverbs 3:9 –

Money isn't everything. For instance ... it isn't plentiful.

– Anonymous –

{ Motivation }

Mo–ti–va–tion /ˌməʊtɪˈveɪʃən/ *noun*

1. The act or process of motivating. 2. The state of being motivated. 3. Something that motivates; an incentive. 4. Inspiration.

Let us think of ways to motivate one
another to acts of love and good works.
– Hebrews 10:24 –

There is no condemnation for
those who belong to Christ Jesus.
– Romans 8:1 –

The LORD is my inheritance;
therefore, I will hope in Him!
– Lamentations 3:24 –

People often say that motivation doesn't last.
Well, neither does bathing – that's why we
recommend it daily.

– Zig Ziglar –

{ Obedience }

O–be–di–ence/əˈbiːdɪəns/*noun*

1. The quality or condition of being obedient.
2. The act of obeying. 3. Submission, compliance.

You must fully obey the LORD our God
and follow all His laws and commands.
Continue to obey in the future as you do now.
– *1 Kings 8:61 NCV* –

The answer is in Jesus Christ our Lord.
So you see how it is: In my mind
I really want to obey God's law.
– *Romans 7:25* –

Obey God's message!
Don't fool yourselves by just listening to it.
– *James 1:22 CEV* –

God will never reveal more truth about Himself
till you obey what you know already.
– Oswald Chambers –

{ Parents }

Par-ents /ˈpɛərənts/ *noun*

1. Those who beget, give birth to, or nurture and raise a child, being either a father or mother. 2. Guardian.

Honor your father and mother.
Then you will live a long life in the
land the LORD your God is giving you.
– *Exodus 20:12* –

My child, obey the teachings of your parents.
– *Proverbs 1:8* CEV –

Children, you belong to the Lord, and you do
the right thing when you obey your parents.
– *Ephesians 6:1* CEV –

Always remember that the best things in life aren't things.

– Anonymous –

{ Patience }

Pa–tience/'peɪʃəns/*noun*

1. The capacity, quality, or fact of being patient. 2. Tolerance, forbearance.

I waited patiently for the LORD to help me,
and He turned to me and heard my cry.
– Psalm 40:1 –

Be patient with each other, making allowance
for each other's faults because of your love.
– Ephesians 4:2 –

If we look forward to something we don't yet
have, we must wait patiently and confidently.
– Romans 8:25 –

Patience is the companion of wisdom.
— St. Augustine —

{ Peers }

Peers/pɪəs/*noun*

1. People who have equal standing with
another or others, as in rank, class, or age.

Do not be fooled: Bad friends
will ruin good habits.
– *1 Corinthians 15:33 NCV* –

Follow only what is good. Remember that those
who do good prove that they are God's children.
– *3 John 1:11* –

Keep company with God and learn a life of love.
– *Ephesians 5:1 MSG* –

Do you have a strong will or a strong won't?
– John L. Mason –

{ Perfection }

Per–fec–tion /pəˈfɛkʃən/ *noun*

1. The quality or condition of being perfect.
2. The act or process of perfecting. 3. A person or thing considered to be perfect. 4. Excellence, flawlessness, precision, exactness.

God's way is perfect. All the LORD's
promises prove true. He is a shield
for all who look to Him for protection.
– 2 Samuel 22:31 –

Let your patience show itself perfectly in
what you do. Then you will be perfect and
complete and will have everything you need.
– James 1:4 NCV –

What matters is not your outer
appearance – the styling of your hair,
the jewelry you wear, the cut of
your clothes – but your inner disposition.
– 1 Peter 3:1 MSG –

Don't try to be perfect; just be an excellent
example of a human being.

– Anthony Robbins –

{ Popularity }

Pop-u-lar-i-ty/ˈpɒpjʊlærɪtɪ/*noun*

1. The quality or state of being popular, especially the state of being widely admired, accepted, or sought after. 2. Favor, fame, esteem, acclaim, status, reputation.

"There's trouble ahead when you live
only for the approval of others, saying
what flatters them, doing what indulges them.
Popularity contests are not truth contests."
– *Luke 6:26* MSG –

Make every effort to give yourself to
God as the kind of person He will approve.
– *2 Timothy 2:15* NCV –

Follow the example of those who
are going to inherit God's promises
because of their faith and endurance.
– *Hebrews 6:12* –

Seek not the favor of the multitude; it is
seldom got by honest and lawful means. But
seek the testimony of few; and number not
voices, but weigh them.

– Immanuel Kant –

{ Prayer }

Pray–er/prɛə/*noun*

1. Words that one says to God to give thanks, to ask for help or share one's heart. 2. A reverent petition made to God. 3. An act of communion with God. 4. Worship, devotion, appeal, request, two-way communication.

The earnest prayer of a righteous person has great power and produces wonderful results.
– *James 5:16* –

"Ask, and you will receive.
Search, and you will find.
Knock, and the door will be opened for you."
– *Matthew 7:7* CEV –

Never stop praying.
– *1 Thessalonians 5:17* –

Keep praying in order to get a better understanding of God Himself.
– Oswald Chambers –

{ Priorities }

Pri-or-i-ties /praɪˈɒrɪtɪs/ *noun*

1. Precedence, especially established by order of importance or urgency. 2. Something afforded or deserving prior attention.

"Love the Lord your God with all your
passion and prayer and intelligence.
This is the most important, the first on any list."
– *Matthew 22:37 MSG* –

"Your heart will always
be where your treasure is."
– *Matthew 6:21 CEV* –

"You can't worship two gods at once.
Loving one god, you'll end up hating the other.
Adoration of one feeds contempt for the other."
– *Matthew 6:24 MSG* –

Lord, we don't mind who is second as long as
You are first.

– W. E. Stangter –

{ Protection }

Pro-tec-tion/prəˈtɛkʃən/*noun*

1. The act of protecting. 2. The condition of
being protected. 3. Defense, security, shelter,
safety.

Even when I walk through the darkest valley,
I will not be afraid, for You are close beside me.
Your rod and Your staff protect and comfort me.
– *Psalm 23:4* –

Protect me as You would Your very own eyes;
hide me in the shadow of Your wings.
– *Psalm 17:8* CEV –

The LORD says, "I will rescue those who love
Me. I will protect those who trust in My name."
– *Psalm 91:14* –

God's angels often protect His servants from
potential enemies.

– Billy Graham –

{ Provision }

Pro–vi–sion /prə'vɪʒən/ *noun*

1. The act of supplying or fitting out. 2. Something provided. 3. A preparatory action or measure.

> "Your Father knows the things
> you need before you ask Him."
> – *Matthew 6:8* NCV –

God can give you more blessings than you need.
Then you will always have plenty of everything.
– *2 Corinthians 9:8* NCV –

Don't get tired of helping others.
You will be rewarded when the time is right.
– *Galatians 6:9* CEV –

A great burden falls away if we let God run the universe.

– Robert Cummings –

{ Purity }

Pu–ri–ty/ˈpjʊərɪtɪ/*noun*

1. The quality or condition of being pure.
2. Freedom from sin or guilt. 3. Innocence, goodness.

We prove ourselves by our purity, our understanding, our patience, our kindness, by the Holy Spirit within us, and by our sincere love.
– *2 Corinthians 6:6* –

How can a young person live a pure life?
By obeying Your word.
– *Psalm 119:9 NCV* –

Run from anything that stimulates youthful lusts. Instead, pursue righteous living, faithfulness, love, and peace. Enjoy the companionship of those who call on the Lord with pure hearts.
– *2 Timothy 2:22* –

There are no better cosmetics than a severe temperance and purity, modesty and humility, a gracious temper and calmness of spirit.
– John Ruskin –

{ Purpose }

Pur-pose/ ˈpɜːpəs /*noun*

1. The object toward which one strives or for which something exists. 2. A result or effect that is intended or desired. 3. Aim, goal, intention.

"I have spared you for a purpose –
to show you My power and to spread
My fame throughout the earth."
– *Exodus 9:16* –

God causes everything to work together
for the good of those who love God and
are called according to His purpose for them.
– *Romans 8:28* –

The LORD will work out His plans for my life –
for Your faithful love, O LORD, endures forever.
– *Psalm 138:8* –

The main thing in this world is not being sure what God's will is, but seeking it sincerely, and following what we do understand of it.
— Paul Tournier —

{ **Reassurance** }

Re-as-sur-ance /ˌriː əˈʃʊərəns/ *noun*

1. The act of reassuring; restoring someone's confidence. 2. Support, comfort, assurance, guarantee.

"I am the LORD your God, who holds your right hand, and I tell you, 'Don't be afraid. I will help you.'"
– *Isaiah 41:13* NCV –

Give your worries to the LORD, and He will take care of you.
– *Psalm 55:22* NCV –

We know that God is always at work for the good of everyone who loves Him.
– *Romans 8:28* CEV –

God always gives His best to those who leave the choice with Him.

– Jim Elliot –

{ Relationships }

Re-la-tion-ships/ rɪˈleɪʃənʃɪps /*noun*

1. The condition or fact of being related. 2. Connection by blood or marriage. 3. A particular type of connection existing between people related to or having dealings with each other. 4. Kinship, connection, association, goodwill, closeness, companionship, friendliness.

We can rejoice in our wonderful
new relationship with God because our
Lord Jesus Christ has made us friends of God.
– Romans 5:11 –

Isn't it obvious that your GOD is
present with you; that He has given you
peaceful relations with everyone around?
– 1 Chronicles 22:18 MSG –

"A person is a fool to store up earthly wealth
but not have a rich relationship with God."
– Luke 12:21 –

> You can never establish a personal
> relationship without opening up your own
> heart.
>
> – Paul Tournier –

{ Relaxation }

Re-lax-a-tion/ˌriːlækˈseɪʃən/*noun*

1. The act of relaxing or the state of being relaxed. 2. Refreshment of body or mind. 3. Recreation, leisure, rest.

"Come to Me, all of you who are weary and carry heavy burdens, and I will give you rest."
– *Matthew 11:28* –

God's a sanctuary during bad times.
The moment you arrive, you relax;
you're never sorry you knocked.
– *Psalm 9:9* MSG –

I find rest in God; only He can save me.
He is my rock and my salvation.
He is my defender; I will not be defeated.
– *Psalm 62:1-2* NCV –

Leisure is time for doing something useful.
– Benjamin Franklin –

{ Reliability }

Re-li-a-bil-i-ty/ rɪˈlaɪəbəlɪtɪ/*noun*

1. The quality of being dependable or reliable.
2. Dependability, consistency, trustworthiness.

Reliable friends who do what they say are
like cool drinks in sweltering heat – refreshing!
– *Proverbs 25:13 MSG* –

The LORD watches over those who fear Him,
those who rely on His unfailing love.
– *Psalm 33:18* –

God, You won't drop me,
You'll never let me down.
– *Psalm 31:3 MSG* –

Be like a postage stamp. Stick to one thing
until you get there.

– Josh Billings –

{ Reputation }

Rep-u-ta-tion /ˌrɛpjʊˈteɪʃən/ *noun*

1. The general estimation in which a person is held by others. 2. The state or situation of being held in high esteem. 3. A specific characteristic or trait ascribed to a person or thing. 4. Character, status, standing.

Never let loyalty and kindness leave you!
Then you will find favor with both God
and people, and you will earn a good reputation.
– Proverbs 3:3-4 –

A good reputation and respect are
worth much more than silver and gold.
– Proverbs 22:1 CEV –

Always let others see you behaving properly, even
though they may still accuse you of doing wrong.
– 1 Peter 2:12 CEV –

Reputation is what men and women think
of us; character is what God and the angels
know of us.

– Thomas Paine –

{ Respect }

Re–spect/rɪˈspɛkt/*verb*/*noun*

1. To feel or show deferential regard for.
2. A feeling of appreciation. 3. The state of being regarded with honor. 4. Willingness to show consideration or appreciation.
5. Esteem, reverence.

Respect everyone and show
special love for God's people.
– *1 Peter 2:17* CEV –

A person with good sense is respected.
– *Proverbs 13:15* –

Show respect to old people; stand up in their
presence. Show respect also to your God.
– *Leviticus 19:32* NCV –

Without respect, love cannot go far or rise
high; it is an angel with but one wing.
– Alexandre Dumas –

{ Responsibility }

Re–spon–si–bil–i–ty /rɪˌspɒnsəˈbɪlɪtɪ/ *noun*

1. The state, quality, or fact of being responsible. 2. Something for which one is responsible. 3. Duty, obligation, burden, accountability, task.

God has given me the responsibility of serving His church by proclaiming His entire message.
– *Colossians 1:25* –

"You have been faithful in handling this small amount, so now I will give you many more responsibilities."
– *Matthew 25:21* –

Each person must be responsible for himself.
– *Galatians 6:5 NCV* –

The only exercise some people get is jumping at conclusions, running down their friends, sidestepping responsibility, and pushing their luck.

– Arnold Glasow –

{ Rules }

Rules/ruːls/*noun*

1. Governing power or its possession or use.
2. An authoritative, prescribed direction
for conduct, especially one of the regulations
governing procedure in a legislative body or
a regulation observed by the players in a game,
sport, or contest. 3. Regulation, principle, law.

"Obey My laws and rules; a person who obeys
them will live because of them. I am the LORD."
– Leviticus 18:5 NCV –

The rules of the LORD can be trusted;
they make plain people wise.
– Psalm 19:7 NCV –

Happy are those who keep His rules,
who try to obey Him with their whole heart.
– Psalm 119:2 NCV –

Obedience is the means whereby we show the
earnestness of our desire to do God's will.
– Oswald Chambers –

{ Salvation }

Sal–va–tion /sæl'veɪʃən/ *noun*

1. The belief that God saves people by providing eternal life. 2. Preservation or deliverance from destruction, difficulty, or evil. 3. A source, means, or cause of such preservation or deliverance. 4. Deliverance by redemption from the power of sin and from the penalties ensuing from it. 5. Redemption, rescue, atonement.

Jesus is the only One who can save people.
No one else in the world is able to save us.
– Acts 4:12 NCV –

Salvation is not a reward for the good things
we have done, so none of us can boast about it.
– Ephesians 2:9 –

Work hard to show the results of your salvation,
obeying God with deep reverence and fear. For
God is working in you, giving you the desire
and the power to do what pleases Him.
– Philippians 2:12-13 –

Salvation is God's way of making us real people.

— St. Augustine —

{ School }

School/skuːl/*noun*

1. An institution for the instruction of children or people under college age. 2. A division of an educational institution constituting several grades or classes. 3. The process of being educated formally.

If you have good sense, instruction will help you to have even better sense. And if you live right, education will help you to know even more.
– *Proverbs 9:9* CEV –

Let instruction and knowledge mean more to you than silver or the finest gold.
– *Proverbs 8:10* CEV –

Start with God – the first step in learning is bowing down to GOD.
– *Proverbs 1:7* MSG –

Anyone who stops learning is old, whether at twenty or eighty. Anyone who keeps learning stays young. The greatest thing in life is to keep your mind young.

– Henry Ford –

{ Security }

Se–cu–ri–ty/sɪˈkjʊərɪtɪ/*noun*

1. Freedom from risk or danger. 2. Freedom from doubt, anxiety, or fear. 3. Safety, confidence, protection.

The LORD is my rock, my fortress,
and my savior; my God is my rock, in
whom I find protection. He is my shield,
the power that saves me, and my place of safety.
– *Psalm 18:2* –

Trust in the LORD and do good. Then you
will live safely in the land and prosper.
– *Psalm 37:3* –

I will say to the LORD, "You are
my place of safety and protection.
You are my God and I trust You."
– *Psalm 91:2 NCV* –

In His love He clothes us, enfolds us and
embraces; that tender love completely
surrounds us, never to leave us.
– Julian of Norwich –

{ Self-esteem }

Self–es–teem/sɛlfɪ'stiːm/*noun*

1. Pride in oneself. 2. Self-respect, self-worth, confidence.

I praise You because You made me in an amazing and wonderful way. What You have done is wonderful. I know this very well.
– Psalm 139:14 NCV –

And this is the boldness we have in God's presence: that if we ask God for anything that agrees with what He wants, He hears us.
– 1 John 5:14 NCV –

We are God's masterpiece. He has created us anew in Christ Jesus.
– Ephesians 2:10 –

He can who thinks he can, and he can't who thinks he can't. This is an inexorable, indisputable law.

— Henry Ford —

{ Siblings }

Sib–lings /ˈsɪblɪŋs/ *noun*

1. A person's brothers or sisters. 2. Family, relative.

It's better to have a partner than go it alone.
Share the work, share the wealth.
And if one falls down, the other helps.
– Ecclesiastes 4:9-10 MSG –

"Treat others as you want them to treat you."
– Matthew 7:12 CEV –

Work at getting along with
each other and with God.
– Hebrews 12:15 MSG –

The art of a good relationship is to value
differences, build on strengths and
compensate for weaknesses.

– Stephen R. Covey –

{ Socializing }

So-cial-i-zing/ˈsəʊʃəˌlaɪzɪŋ/*noun*

1. The act of meeting for social purposes.
2. Mix, mingle, party.

Don't hang out with angry people;
don't keep company with hotheads.
– *Proverbs 22:24 MSG* –

Spend time with the wise
and you will become wise.
– *Proverbs 13:20 NCV* –

Post a guard at my mouth, GOD,
set a watch at the door of my lips.
Don't let me so much as dream of evil
or thoughtlessly fall into bad company.
– *Psalm 141:3 MSG* –

To know someone here or there with whom
you can feel there is understanding in spite of
differences or thoughts expressed ... that can
make life a garden.

– Johann Wolfgang von Goethe –

{ Stress }

Stress /strɛs/ *noun*

1. A mentally or emotionally disruptive or upsetting condition occurring in response to adverse external influences and capable of affecting physical health. 2. Anxiety, worry, tension.

As pressure and stress bear down on me,
I find joy in Your commands.
– *Psalm 119:143* –

"When you go through deep waters,
I will be with you. When you go through
rivers of difficulty, you will not drown."
– *Isaiah 43:2* –

God is our mighty fortress, always
ready to help in times of trouble.
– *Psalm 46:1* CEV –

Sometimes the Lord calms the storm;
sometimes He lets the storm rage and calms
His child.

– Anonymous –

{ Success }

Suc–cess /sək'sɛs/ *noun*

1. The achievement of something desired, planned, or attempted. 2. The gaining of fame or prosperity. 3. Triumph, victory, conquest, accomplishment.

The LORD will make you the head
and not the tail, and you will always
be on top and never at the bottom.
– *Deuteronomy 28:13* –

May God grant your heart's desires
and make all your plans succeed.
– *Psalm 20:4* –

Lord our God, treat us well. Give us success
in what we do; yes, give us success in what we do.
– *Psalm 90:17* NCV –

People rarely succeed unless they have fun in what they are doing.

– Dale Carnegie –

{ Support }

Sup–port/sə'pɔːt/verb/*noun*

1. To bear the weight of. 2. To hold in position so as to keep from falling, sinking, or slipping. 3. To keep from weakening or failing. 4. The act of supporting. 5. Assist, assistance, help, aid.

O God, pledge Your support for me.
Give it to me in writing, with Your signature.
You're the only one who can do it!
– *Job 17:3* MSG –

You have given me Your shield
of victory. Your right hand supports
me; Your help has made me great.
– *Psalm 18:35* –

The LORD supported me. He led
me to a place of safety; He rescued
me because He delights in me.
– *2 Samuel 22:19-20* –

We must support one another, console one another, mutually help, counsel, and advise.
— Thomas à Kempis —

{ Talents }

Tal-ents /ˈtælənts/ *noun*

1. A marked innate ability, as for artistic accomplishment. 2. Natural endowment or ability of a superior quality. 3. Aptitude, gift, ability.

God has given us different
gifts for doing certain things well.
– *Romans 12:6* –

"To those who use well what they
are given, even more will be given,
and they will have an abundance."
– *Matthew 25:29* –

Each of you has been blessed with one of
God's many wonderful gifts to be used in
the service of others. So use your gift well.
– *1 Peter 4:10* CEV –

Your talent is God's gift to you. What you do
with it is your gift back to God.

– Leo Buscaglia –

{ Thoughtfulness }

Thought–ful–ness/ˈθɔːtfʊlnɪs/*noun*

1. Having or showing concern for the well-being of others. 2. Consideration, contemplation, meditation.

Our LORD, everything You do
is kind and thoughtful.
– *Psalm 145:17* CEV –

You must get along with each other.
You must learn to be considerate of
one another, cultivating a life in common.
– *1 Corinthians 1:10* MSG –

Be good to each other and to everyone else.
– *1 Thessalonians 5:15* CEV –

Be careful of your thoughts: they may become words at any moment.

– Ira Gassen –

{ Trust }

Trust /trʌst/ *noun/verb*

1. Firm reliance on the integrity, ability, or character of a person. 2. Something committed into the care of another. 3. Reliance on something in the future. 4. To be confident. 5. To believe. 6. Faith, belief, hope, expectation.

But when I am afraid, I will put my trust in You.
I praise God for what He has promised.
I trust in God, so why should I be afraid?
– Psalm 56:3-4 –

I trust Your love, and I feel like
celebrating because You rescued me.
– Psalm 13:5 CEV –

Those who know the LORD trust Him, because
He will not leave those who come to Him.
– Psalm 9:10 NCV –

Trust the past to God's mercy, the present to His love, and the future to His providence.
— St. Augustine —

{ Uniqueness }

U–nique–ness/juːˈniːknɪs/*noun*

1. The quality of being one of a kind. 2. Individuality, exclusivity, rareness.

You will be My own special treasure
from among all the peoples on earth.
– *Exodus 19:5* –

How precious are Your
thoughts about me, O God.
– *Psalm 139:17* –

I will give you a good name, a name of
distinction, among all the nations of the earth.
– *Zephaniah 3:20* –

A wonderful realization will be the day you
realize that you are unique in all the world.
– Leo Buscaglia –

{ Values }

Val–ues/ˈvæljuːs/*noun*

1. A principle, standard, or quality considered worthwhile or desirable. 2. Worth, importance, principles, standards, morals, ethics, ideals.

Don't be like the people of this world,
but let God change the way you think.
Then you will know how to do everything
that is good and pleasing to Him.
– *Romans 12:2* CEV –

Don't love the world or anything
that belongs to the world. If you love
the world, you cannot love the Father.
– *1 John 2:15* CEV –

We must live decent lives for all to see. Don't let
yourself think about ways to indulge yourself.
– *Romans 13:13-14* –

Try not to become a person of success, but
rather a person of value.

– Albert Einstein –

{ Wisdom }

Wis–dom/ˈwɪzdəm/*noun*

1. The ability to discern or judge what is true, right, or lasting. 2. The sum of learning through the ages. 3. A wise outlook, plan, or course of action. 4. Insight, knowledge, understanding, intelligence.

To one person the Spirit gives the ability to give wise advice; to another the same Spirit gives a message of special knowledge.
– 1 Corinthians 12:8 –

Wise people have great power, and those with knowledge have great strength.
– Proverbs 24:5 NCV –

It is not just older people who are wise; they are not the only ones who understand what is right.
– Job 32:9 NCV –

One can have knowledge without having wisdom, but one cannot have wisdom without having knowledge.

– R. C. Sproul –

{ Words }

Words/wɜːdz/*noun*

1. A sound or a combination of sounds, or its representation in writing or printing, that symbolizes and communicates a meaning.

The right word at the right time
is like precious gold set in silver.
– Proverbs 25:11 CEV –

Giving the right answer at the
right time makes everyone happy.
– Proverbs 15:23 CEV –

"The words you have said will be used to judge
you. Some of your words will prove you right,
but some of your words will prove you guilty."
– Matthew 12:37 NCV –

Words must be weighed, not counted.
– Polish Proverb –

{ Worthiness }

Worth-i-ness/ˈwɜːðɪnɪs/*noun*

1. Having worth, merit, or value. 2. Dignity, honorable, admirable, deserving.

Learn to appreciate and give dignity to your body, not abusing it, as is so common among those who know nothing of God.
– *1 Thessalonians 4:4-5 MSG* –

God created human beings in His own image.
– *Genesis 1:27* –

God put our bodies together in such a way that even the parts that seem the least important are valuable.
– *1 Corinthians 12:24 CEV* –

True dignity is never gained by place, and never lost when honors are withdrawn.
– Phillip Massinger –

The Word of God on Words

A word aptly spoken is like
apples of gold in settings of silver.
Prov. 25:11 NIV

Let my words and my thoughts
be pleasing to you, Lord.
Ps. 19:14 CEV

The words of the wise bring them praise.
Eccles. 10:12 NCV

Saying the right word at
the right time is so pleasing.
Prov. 15:23 NCV

Words kill, words give life; they're either poison or fruit – you choose.

Prov. 18:21 MSG

Wise words bring many benefits.

Prov. 12:14

Gentle words are a tree of life.

Prov. 15:4

Kind words are like honey – sweet to the soul and healthy to the body.

Prov. 16:24

Words That Have Touched My Heart ...

_____

_____

_____

_____

_____

_____

_____

_____

_____

_____

_____